THE CHILTERNS

HISTORIC HOUSES, TOWNS AND VILLAGES

Cottages and church, Ellesborough

SALMON

An Ambassador Book

River Thames at Marlow

INTRODUCTION

The Chilterns Hills range in a south-westerly direction from Bedfordshire, through Hertfordshire and Buckinghamshire, and end in Oxfordshire just above Pangbourne. Here the waters of the Thames thrust through the Goring gap, which separates the Chilterns from the Berkshire Downs. To the north-west is spread the Vale of Aylesbury, with its immense patchwork of fields and hedgerows. To the south and east are the wooded slopes of the Thames, the verdant valley of the little River Chess and the commons around Gerrards Cross.

The Anglo Saxon word 'boc', from which Buckinghamshire derives its name, means simply 'beech tree' and the beech-woods of the Chilterns indeed form its chief feature. Much woodland still remains, clothing the slopes within whose folds nestle numerous delightful villages and small towns with the timber-framing and brick architecture so typical of the area.

There is evidence of man's occupation since earliest times and the ancient trackway known as the Ickfield Way follows the line of the Chiltern escarpment. Remains from Roman, Saxon and Norman times are, however, scanty and the area's architectural heritage can be found in the fine range of domestic buildings, a collection of beautiful medieval churches and a number of superb manor houses and historic homes, including Cliveden, Stonor, Chenies and West Wycombe.

Buckinghamshire also has many historical and literary connections; amongst the figures with whom the county is associated are Disraeli, John Milton, John Hampden of Civil War fame, William Penn and the poet Thomas Gray.

The Chilterns may be close to London and the other large centres of population along the Thames valley, yet they retain an atmosphere of unspoilt rural charm, where it is easy to lose oneself among sleepy villages, leafy lanes and small market towns.

HISTORIC HOUSES

Stonor Park. Situated at the foot of the Chiltern hills in Oxfordshire, the house is set in a magnificent deer park. Although it now appears mainly 18th century in style, the history of Stonor Park pre-dates that by some five hundred years. An arcade of arches which was part of the original hall has survived and the chapel, with its alternating layers of brick and tile, dates from the 14th century. The Stonor family was distinguished in public affairs for many generations but in Tudor times their firm allegiance to the Church of Rome brought persecution and loss of office. The house became a centre for Catholic learning with a remarkable library but it was not until the 1830s, in more tolerant times, that they were able to resume their public role.

Princes Risborough Manor. *(top)* In the centre of the village, off the market square near the church, stands the 17th century manor house at Princes Risborough. Now owned by the National Trust, this fine red-brick mansion is noted for its Jacobean oak staircase and 18th century wainscoting.

Chenies Manor. *(bottom)* With its twisting chimneys and mullioned windows this superb red-brick manor house dates from Tudor times when it was the home of the Russell family, the Dukes of Bedford. At that time it was considerable larger, since what remains today is only one wing of the original mansion. In the 17th century the family moved from Chenies Manor to another family home, Woburn Abbey in Bedfordshire, but although the manor house fell into disrepair, some of the Russells were still living in Chenies village in the early years of the 20th century.

Cliveden House. *(top)* Set on cliffs 200 feet above the Thames, Cliveden is the third house to be built on this spectacular site. Frederick, Prince of Wales and father of George II, lived in the original house and here he was entertained by the first ever performance of "Rule Britannia". The present building dates from 1851 when Sir Charles Barry, the architect of the House of Commons, was employed to rebuild Cliveden after a fire. Queen Victoria visited the imposing mansion on a number of occasions and later it became a centre of political activity. The grounds were designed by Capability Brown.

West Wycombe Park. *(bottom)* Standing in a magnificent park, West Wycombe House is an impressive Palladian-style mansion. It owes much of its splendid appearance to Sir Francis Dashwood, MP and Chancellor of the Exchequer, who undertook extensive rebuilding work in the mid-18th century. The grounds, landscaped by Humphrey Repton, include a lake which was created by damming the River Wye. West Wycombe became notorious as the centre of Dashwood's "Hell Fire Club".

Hughenden. Home from 1847 to 1881 to Benjamin Disraeli, who was twice Prime Minister under Queen Victoria, Hughenden Manor stands in a vast 169 acre estate. The mansion dates from Jacobean times but in the 1860s Disraeli undertook considerable alterations both to the exterior, which was refaced, and to the interior, which he transformed in Victorian Gothic style. The house, which is now owned by the National Trust, stands in delightful formal gardens and in it are preserved many of Disraeli's books and other relics of his life as a politician and statesman.

THE CHILTERN HILLS

Bradenham Woods. *(facing)* In pre-historic times the Chiltern hills were covered with a vast forest and much of the area is still rich in beautiful beechwoods. In Bradenham Woods the trees are interspersed with glades, running streams and footpaths which thread between the trees making this a paradise for walkers.

Ellesborough. *(right)* The village of Ellesborough lies some two and a half miles west of Wendover near the line of the ancient Icknield Way. The church, with its impressive tower, is frequently used by visitors to Chequers, the Prime Minister's nearby country retreat. From its position high on a mound, the church offers sweeping views across the Vale of Aylesbury. This is superb walking country, surrounded by the gentle Chiltern landscape, dotted with beechwoods. Nearby is the ancient fort known as Cymbeline's Mount as well as two of the highest points of the Chiltern ridge; Beacon Hill and Pulpit Hill, both over 800 feet.

Burnham Beeches. It was through the far-sightedness of a Victorian naturalist, F. G. Heath, that 400 acres of this beautiful beech-wood, occupying the Buckinghamshire side of the River Thames, was preserved for public use. It was bought in 1880 by the Corporation of London which began a conservation programme resulting in the flourishing and well-maintained woodland which exists today. Winding between the ancient beech trees there are numerous leafy walks some of which are named after local landowners or famous people. Among them is Mendelssohn's Slope, a grassy valley visited and much loved by the composer on his visits to England in the 1830s and 1840s.

Turville Mill. *(top)* Behind the village of Turville, west of High Wycombe near the Oxfordshire border, stands a fine smock mill. Situated on a grassy slope, it offers panoramic views of the Chiltern countryside. The mill, which is now converted into a private dwelling, appeared in the children's film *Chitty Chitty Bang Bang*.

Coombe Hill. *(bottom)* One of several vantage points in the area, offering magnificent views across the Vale of Aylesbury, Coombe Hill is the highest point in the Chiltern hills at 825 feet. It was given to the National Trust in 1912 by Lord Lee, the benefactor who also presented Chequers, now the official country residence of the Prime Minister, to the nation. A distinctive monument was erected on the top of the hill in 1904 to honour all those who lost their lives during the South African War.

Hughenden Valley. *(right)* Running northwards from High Wycombe, flanked by the rolling slopes of the Chilterns, the Hughenden Valley is dotted with farms and hamlets. At the southern end of the valley is Hughenden Manor, home of Benjamin Disraeli who was Prime Minister under Queen Victoria. When Disraeli bought the estate in 1847 he remodelled the grounds and introduced a tree-planting scheme. Within the estate stands the church where the statesman is buried.

Pitstone Mill. *(facing)* One of a number of unspoilt Buckinghamshire villages, each with its ancient stone church, Pitstone is situated near Ivinghoe Beacon. At nearby Pitstone Green stands one of the oldest post mills in Britain. It was built in about 1627 to grind grain and completely restored in the 19th century. Although it is no longer in use, the two sets of millstones are still in position.

PICTURESQUE VILLAGES

Long Crendon. A village of thatched cottages, timber-framed houses and mellow stone walls, Long Crendon in Buckinghamshire prospered for 300 years from the needle-making industry. The late 14th century Court House *(facing)* was originally used as a wool store but from the reign of Henry V until recent times manorial courts were held here.

Monks Risborough. *(top)* A mile north of Princes Risborough, a pleasant walk along the Roman Icknield Way, is Monks Risborough. It is an ancient village with a number of picturesque old cottages and a 16th century dovecote. The origin of the village's name is variously attributed to the monks of Canterbury, who once held the manor, to the religious community at nearby Great Missenden or to an association with Notley Abbey.

Latimer. *(bottom)* A picturesque hamlet in the Chess Valley, Latimer is unspoilt. Some of the paths around the tiny village green are paved with Roman tiles found in the vicinity. The village pump and a war memorial stand on the green alongside an unusual memorial to a French horse which was rescued from the Boer Wars by Lord Chesham of Latimer House.

Fingest. Nestling in a secluded valley, the little village of Fingest lies amid fine beech-wood scenery a few miles north of Henley-on-Thames. The ancient Parish Church *(left)*, which dates from the 12th century, is distinguished by the fact that its large Norman tower is surmounted by an unusual double saddleback roof which was added later.

Turville. A perfect example of a Chiltern village, tranquil Turville has many delightful old houses built over the centuries in a pleasing variety of materials. Flint-faced cottages are grouped around a tiny village green near the Norman church *(facing)*. Many other houses exhibit mellow brickwork while the Bull and Butcher Inn, in common with several other buildings nearby, is thatched and half-timbered.

Penn. *(top)* Described by Sir John Betjeman as "the Chelsea of the Chilterns", Penn lies on a high ridge with glorious views over the surrounding beechwoods. Holy Trinity Church dates from the 14th century and contains many monuments to the Penn family whose most famous member is William Penn, the Quaker founder of Pennsylvania. It is claimed that twelve counties can be seen from the church tower. The village pond stands at one corner of the triangular green around which are grouped some attractive 17th century cottages.

Bradenham. *(bottom)* Between High Wycombe and Princes Risborough, the little village of Bradenham nestles in a valley below Bledlow Ridge. The fine 17th century red-brick manor house beside the green was once the home of Isaac Disraeli and his son Benjamin, the future Prime Minister. The village church, with its Norman doorway and Perpendicular style tower, is also of interest. Amongst the 18th century heraldic glass in the north chapel can be seen one of the earliest examples of the use of enamelled glass in the country.

Haddenham. Much of Haddenham's charm lies in the contrast between its wide thoroughfares and its narrow winding streets and pathways, many of which are lined with white walls capped with red pantiles. The 13th century parish church of Saint Mary *(above)* is at the heart of the village, its imposing bell tower looking down on the thatched roof of Church Farm House, a fine half-timbered 15th century building. The pond which laps at the walls of the church was once the centre of a thriving local industry breeding Aylesbury ducks for the table.

Cuddington. *(facing)* On the northern slopes of the Chilterns there are many delightful villages where ancient cottages and Norman or Saxon churches are surrounded by some of England's richest agricultural land. Characteristic of the Chiltern landscape Cuddington, in the Vale of Aylesbury, is one such. This attractive thatched cottage with its little dormer windows looks out across the small village green.

Chenies. *(right)* Situated in the Chess valley in Buckinghamshire, Chenies is an attractive village with a fine green surrounded by old cottages. It owes much of its charm to the Russell family, Dukes of Bedford, who lived here for many years, building a model village in the 1850s to house estate workers. The medieval church has much of interest ranging across the centuries from a Norman font to a hammer-beam roof which is Victorian in origin. It is best known for the Bedford Chapel, a private annex to the church which was built in the early 1500s. It contains a remarkable collection of monuments and tombs relating to the Russells.

Stoke Poges. *(top)* The Church of St. Giles, which is immortalised in Thomas Gray's famous poem, "Elegy in a Country Churchyard", stands a short distance from Stoke Poges village. Set in a tranquil spot surrounded by trees, the church dates from the 13th century with a chapel which was added in 1560. The poet, his mother and other members of his family lie buried in the churchyard and in a nearby field there is a 20 feet high monument to the poet.

Chalfont St. Giles. With its pretty green, pond and ancient church, the village of Chalfont St. Giles is one of the finest in the Chilterns. It contains several noteworthy buildings including the timber and brick house known as Milton's Cottage. *(bottom).* Now kept as a museum, the poet lived here during the plague year of 1665 and it was here he completed 'Paradise Lost' and began 'Paradise Regained'.

West Wycombe. Now owned in its entirety by the National Trust, West Wycombe has many fine buildings spanning the 16th to the 18th centuries. One of the most interesting features of the village is the 15th century Church Loft *(facing)* with its overhanging storey and archway. It was here that the churchwardens met and, to the side of the arch, a doorway leads into a small room which was used as the prison. A lane connects the archway with the church at the top of the hill.

ALONG THE THAMES

Mapledurham. Some of the most outstanding scenery on the River Thames is found at Mapledurham in Oxfordshire where thickly wooded hills fringe the river. The church, half hidden in the trees, the old weir and the mill *(above)* are favourite subjects for artists. The Tudor manor house which stands nearby was used as a setting both by Galsworthy in *The Forsyte Saga* and also by Kenneth Grahame in his *Wind in the Willows*. Mapledurham Watermill is the last working mill on the Thames and is still producing wholemeal flour.

Maidenhead. One of the smartest of Thames-side resorts, Maidenhead stands on a busy section of the Thames. Here the river is crossed by a fine 18th century stone bridge as well as by a viaduct designed by Brunel. From the town there is a half-mile-long promenade alongside the river to busy Boulter's Lock *(top)*. One of the most popular and attractive locks on the river, it is connected by a bridge to a small island.

Bisham. Close to Marlow on the Berkshire bank of the Thames is Bisham Church *(bottom)* with its square Norman tower and distinctive red-tiled roof. A favourite subject for artists and photographers, it stands in a picturesque situation on the banks of the river. Bisham Abbey, a short distance upstream, is the only abbey to have been restored by Henry VIII after the dissolution; he gave it to his fourth wife, Anne of Cleves, as part of her divorce settlement.

Marlow. *(left)* With its graceful bridge, the wide sweep of the weir downstream and the wooded hills upstream, Marlow is acknowledged to be one of the show pieces of the Thames. Marlow Lock, set against the magnificent background of Quarry Woods, has one of the best situations on the river and the soaring spire of the Church of All Saints stands out alongside the elegant suspension bridge which was erected in 1829.

Hambleden. A good starting point for exploring some of the most beautiful valleys in the Chilterns, Hambleden is a picturesque village with an old smithy, some ancient cottages and an impressive church which is approached through a lych-gate. About a mile from the village beside Mill End weir, which is popular with canoeists, stands Hambleden Mill *(facing)*. It dates originally from 1338 and probably no building beside the Thames is more photographed than this handsome structure. At Hambleden the river enters one of its finest stretches as it threads its way past a series of islands between well-wooded banks.

Medmenham. Not far from Marlow on the Buckinghamshire side of the river is the pretty village of Medmenham with its picturesque cottages and ancient church. From the village, Ferry Lane leads down to the river and the site of Medmenham Abbey *(top)*. The original St. Mary's Abbey was an early 13th century Cistercian foundation but the present 18th century ruin is associated with the infamous "Hell Fire Club" lead by Sir Frances Dashwood of West Wycombe House.

Cookham. *(bottom)* A village of considerable beauty and historical interest, Cookham lies on a heavily wooded reach of the Thames in Berkshire. The church conspicuously situated beside the river, has many interesting features. Part Norman, it is mentioned in the Domesday Book and the tower is unusual in that it has both a clock and a sundial. Cookham Lock lies on a superbly wooded section of the river and, beyond the lock cut, four streams of the river are reunited and crossed by a bridge and ferry.

Henley-on-Thames. The River Thames lies at the heart of Henley and some of the finest scenery on the river is found in the area. An ancient town with a history which dates back at least to 1179, Henley attracts both boating enthusiasts and holiday-makers but it is especially known for the world-famous regatta which has been held here annually since 1839. The Old Angel Inn, a favoured halt on the river, stands beside Henley's fine five-arched bridge. The present structure, bearing carvings on the keystones of Father Thames and the goddess Isis, was built in 1786 but it is known that a bridge has spanned the river here since the early 13th century.

BUCKINGHAMSHIRE TOWNS

Wendover. Set in one of the few gaps in the Chilterns, Wendover is an old town which was on the direct coach route from London to Aylesbury and it retains some fine inns, including one where Oliver Cromwell slept. The ancient Icknield Way runs through this area and where it enters the town it briefly becomes Wendover High Street. There are many interesting buildings in the town including a handsome row known as Anne Boleyn's Cottages *(facing)*.

Aylesbury. Surrounded by the superb wooded countryside of the Chilterns, Aylesbury is the county town of Buckinghamshire. Alongside the modern buildings and bustle of the town centre, narrow Tudor alleyways and squares of mellowed houses and inns have been preserved and the tower of the massive 13th century church *(bottom)* is topped by a 17th century spire which is visible for miles. In the Market Square *(top)* there is a fine statue of John Hampden (1594 - 1643), a local man who had a significant role in the events leading up to the Civil War.

Princes Risborough. Standing on the escarpment of the Chiltern Hills, surrounded by rolling fields and woodlands, Princes Risborough is a village of considerable charm. In addition to its Manor House, it has a number of interesting old houses, many of them timbered and thatched. The brick-built, arcaded market house *(top)* has a wooden cupola surmounted by a clock.

Chesham. A lively town which has for generations played an important part in many local industries, Chesham has a long and fascinating history and retains some interesting features from past centuries. Situated in the deep valley of the River Chess, the town is surrounded by steeply rising hills with some of the finest scenery in the county on its doorstep. One of the most picturesque parts of old Chesham is around the Bury, a fine red-brick mansion built in the reign of Queen Anne. Church Street, full of architectural interest, runs from the market square past the Bury to St. Mary's Church *(bottom)*. With a history going back at least to 1150, Chesham's parish church has been much restored but many of the best features have been retained.

Amersham. Surrounded by the beautiful countryside of the Chilterns and the Thames valley, Amersham is divided into the old town and a newer part which sits on the hill which separates the Misbourne and Chess valleys. The streets of Old Amersham are lined with ancient inns and houses and around the Market Square are many picturesque old shops as well as the 17th century Town Hall. A narrow road leads to the St. Mary's Parish Church. Although the flint covering was added during restoration which took place in the 1890s, the church dates from the 13th century. It contains some fine stained glass, a rich collection of monuments and has an unusual little spire on top of the west tower.

GRAND UNION CANAL

Grand Union Canal. Unique among English canals in that it comprises at least eight separate waterways, the Grand Union Canal links London with the industrial cities of the Midlands. Winding through the rolling, wooded scenery of the Chilterns, it reaches Aylesbury *(facing)* where the spacious canal basin is always busy with boats. It was from here in 1832 that the first of many groups of emigrants left England, travelling on narrow boats to Liverpool where they set sail for the New World. The Wendover Arm of the Grand Union Canal *(right)* was originally built for water supply, transferring water from several artesian wells in the area to reservoirs and a pumping station. Now disused, only a short section at the eastern end of the arm is navigable where it joins the main waterway.

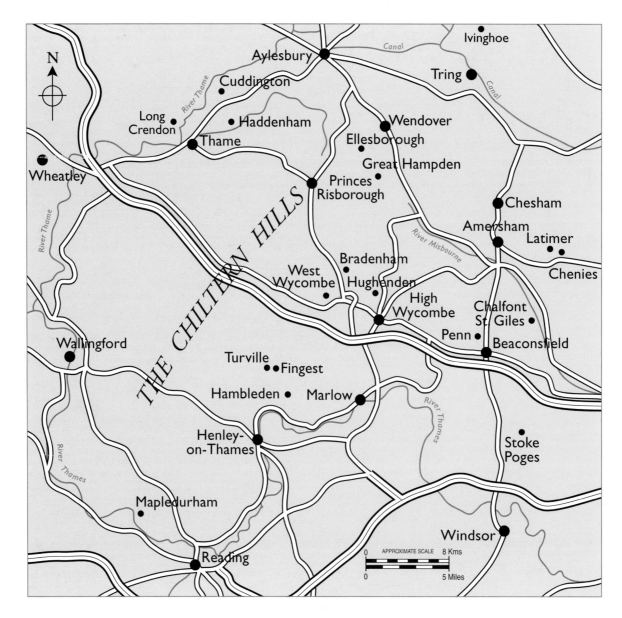

Printed and published by J. Salmon Ltd., Sevenoaks, Kent TN13 1BB

Designed by the Salmon Studio. Copyright © 2000 J. Salmon Ltd.

ISBN 1 902842 09 X

Cover picture: Autumn in the Hughenden Valley   *Back cover:* The Village Green, Chenies